Events and Victims

Bartolomeo Vanzetti
Edited by Jon Curley

PM Press PAMPHLET SERIES

PM Press Pamphlet Series No. 0017
The Young C.L.R. James: A Graphic Novelette
Milton Knight, Lawrence Ware, and Paul Buhle

ISBN: 978-1-62963-514-9

Copyright © 2018
This edition copyright PM Press
All rights reserved

PM Press
PO Box 23912
Oakland, CA 94623
www.pmpress.org

Printed in the USA by the Employee Owners of Thomson-Shore in Dexter, Michigan
www.thomsonshore.com

For Bartolomeo Vanzetti: This project is yours. Late recognition of your literary as well as political vision, which I regard as meager but necessary justice. My gratitude to you for your words and life. I am honored to help bring this work, finally, into the world.

In memory of Grey Space (July 2, 1970–December 4, 2016): friend, anarchist, queer street activist poet

> *only we can see*
> *love when others make nazi*
> *long live anarchy!*

Acknowledgments

Special thanks to Ramsey Kanaan and the whole PM Press staff for their enthusiasm, engagement, and all around helpfulness. My deep appreciation goes to Gregory Nipper and Michael Ryan in particular for their supreme editorial advice and efforts on this project.

I am indebted to many people, those both familiar and exemplary, even some distant stars of illumination beyond the timeline of this work or my own. Let me provide a few names to herald as helpers and healers, shapers, and sharers, of this work and of my thinking about the world in which it exists, past and present: Tom Curley, Hedieh Allameh, Elena Alexander, Gypsy James O'Toole, Michael Heller, Kevin Bradbury, Jane Augustine, Chris Leo, Ariana Curley, Nick Heller, Bobby Lesko, Pam Lamora, Maryam Bahrainian, Pam Rehm, Fanny Howe, Burt Kimmelman, Eric Katz, John Laffey, Eamonn Vitt, the Curleys, the Beauchamps of Braintree, MA, and the illustrious cavalcade of anarchists, socialists, fellow travelers, aligned and non-, revolutionaries and resisters, freethinkers, those for whom a new world is conceivable and for whom the fight is worth taking into the streets and into print. Again and always, ultimate acknowledgment goes to the author, Bartolomeo Vanzetti:

Our Work—Our Lives—Our Pains Nothing! The Taking of Our Lives, Lives of a Good Shoemaker and a Poor Fish Peddler—All! That Last Moment Belongs to Us—That Agony Is Our Triumph!

Introduction
Bartolomeo Vanzetti:
Radical, Prisoner, Prison Writer

"Who can know the incognitos of the future near and remote?"
From a letter of Bartolomeo Vanzetti to Elizabeth Glendower
Evans, May 14, 1926

THE CONTROVERSIAL CASE OF NICOLA SACCO AND BARTOLOMEO VANZETTI, their trial, execution, and legacy, are all well known—"notorious" is the word—resonating even in the present day. More than ninety years ago, two Italian immigrants with anarchist politics were arrested, jailed, and executed for a crime for which evidence was circumstantial at best, doctored at worst, and for which a third party had confessed, testifying that neither individual was involved.

Bartolomeo Vanzetti's courtroom eloquence during his legal trials is well known, and his prison letters are properly acclaimed for offering a constellation of insights about the U.S. prison system, the status of being an immigrant and radical, and the arduous process of becoming educated while incarcerated. Less known—because until now the story had never been published—is that while in prison Vanzetti turned to writing fiction and learning English, completing one short story, "Events and Victims," a blistering condemnation of the intractable economic exploitation of ceaselessly predatory capitalism from an anarchist aesthetic perspective. In this introduction, I wish to address

1

both some of the *incognitos* of Vanzetti's personal and artistic experience and the circumstances surrounding the composition of the story. Some years ago, while reading the 1997 Penguin edition of *The Letters of Sacco and Vanzetti*, I came across a passing reference to a story by Vanzetti, "Events and Victims," and was immediately intrigued. What kind of prisoner undertakes writing, particularly fiction, in a language only recently and partly acquired, under psychological duress, and with the very likely prospect of execution? I discovered that two different manuscript versions of "Events and Victims" existed in the Upton Sinclair papers at the Lilly Library at Indiana University. After reading each version, it occurred to me that Vanzetti's story in some strategically but modestly edited form should be accessible to a wider audience than his prison cells, his tutor in English who edited and advised him on the short story, and the lonely archives of a Midwestern library.

Over the twentieth century, political prisoner writers of all stripes and striations have expressed their visions behind bars, and their words have slipped through those bars, escaping into the freer world, largely to an audience for whom their past experiences and present conditions are unfamiliar. Some of the most remarkable examples include the following: Alexander Berkman's *Prison Memoirs of an Anarchist* (1912), the Italian Marxist Antonio Gramsci's *Prison Notebooks 1929–1935*, American socialist and union leader Eugene Debs's *Walls and Bars* (1927), the Irish revolutionary Countess Constance Markiewicz's *Prison Letters* (1937), *The Autobiography of Malcolm X* (1965), American activist priest Philip Berrigan's *Prison Journals of a Priest Revolutionary* (1970), the prison writer and nationalist George Jackson's *Soledad Brother* (1970), and Nigerian democratic reformer and playwright Wole Soyinka's *The Man Died: Prison Notes* (1972).[1]

Each of these books—a handful among many other titles—is a masterly compression of political analysis, ideological justification, self-evaluation, and historical reflection. They combine the despair and adversity of subjugation with an irrepressible hope in the alteration of the political situation and their own predicament. Their testimonials are the unsanctioned historical documents of outsiders who, embedded within the physical domain of the state, are in fact the insiders. Their critiques and memoirs are often radical, internalized critiques of the system, counterarguments and acts of resistance that serve as blistering refusals, a deconstruction of official, institutional missions and methods.

Prisons make fine mental prophylactics.[2] How impressive the prisoner who learns how to read and write or develop limited literacy skills, especially in a foreign language, while imprisoned. Serving time or awaiting death, possessing the stamina to overcome the distractions of the unsettling nature of the all-too-settled prison cell to devote oneself to a life-affirming industry is superhuman in the face of the dehumanizing. Bartolomeo Vanzetti is the quintessence of a rare talent, sustaining himself through words and beginning to forge a voice in writing under extreme conditions and under the watch of prison guards.

Written by an individual coming *subalternus*, an imprisoned immigrant fishmonger and anarchist who had eked out a modest existence on the fringes of the mainstream, "Events and Victims" emerges as an even more unique instance of marginal literature. While not published as its author had hoped—Vanzetti described its imminent arrival in print to a number of correspondents, including Upton Sinclair, author of numerous social protest novels, including *Boston* (1928), about the Sacco-Vanzetti case, even addressing "my reader" in the first sentence—"Events and Victims" stands as a graphic depiction of dire working conditions reflective of its real world counterpart. It is also a remarkable testament of empowerment for a writer developing his fluency in a new language and, despite circumstances, relentlessly depicting social and economic oppression as a caveat, corrective, and gruelingly, perhaps, prophecy.

"Events and Victims" is a medium-length short story, hardly the "novella" Vanzetti considered it. Whether the term was used erroneously as a diminutive form of novel or he had ambitions to broaden its scope is unknown. A simple tale chronicling the expectations and destinies of ambitious unskilled laborers and their misfortunes at a munitions manufacturing plant, it is a classical quest narrative translated into a modern fable of capitalistic oppression. The framing of Vanzetti's allegorical world is descriptively evasive: set in a country of unspecified geography, New Liberia, and of no certain time frame.[3] However, this imperiled locale, beset by extensive soil erosion on its eastern and western coasts, describes a recognizable atmosphere, certainly for anyone who has labored or lived in dangerous, dirty, and oppressive conditions.

In choosing to name this country New Liberia, Vanzetti shrewdly alludes to the African nation forged by freed American slaves in a state of structural inequality between the ruling Amero-Liberians and native population. Additionally, he ironizes the relationship of the country's beleaguered working citizens to their residence: New Liberty is Old Slavery writ large.

War with Germany benefits the heavy industry of this neutral country and the recruitment of workers to forge weapons of mass destruction compels the narrator and his accomplice Johnny to head to Greenland. The domain is described as a soul-crushing throwback to pre–Industrial Revolution Europe:

> This village is one of the very many industrial feudal tenures scattered amid the forests along the river's banks and the coast of New Liberia. It bears the name of the Overlord who owns by law the two churches, the two factories, and almost all of the houses and the soil itself.

Although archaically described, it could also be a fictional version of an American company town of Vanzetti's own time. Its name too contradicts the actual habitat, an environmentally ruinous realm of infectious disease and ecological blight:

> It is civilization, it is prosperity—which Johnny says "makes the paupers live"—that projects poisons into the air and water, driving out everything that is not artificial. But can man—man who is the most sensitive and delicate of creatures—thrive and rise where the very birds, mice, insects, and plants are unable to exist?

Vanzetti's letters repeatedly express a passionate, protective affection for Nature; indeed, he insisted that his politics were the logical extension of the harmonic relationships he attributed to the natural world and the normative condition of humanity in terms of natural law—cooperative, dynamic, unchecked freedom.

The two laborers find ready employment at the plant, separating soon thereafter into different sectors, only to unite at the story's end, where they are witnesses to a terrible, inevitable workplace accident. The narrative arc is not dramatic, the story in general formulaic; the action enveloped within the chaotic climax, in light of the narrator's commentary throughout—a combination of careful critique and scornful polemic—is predictable, yet no less affecting. Moreover, the massing of social observation, philosophical musing, and almost anthropologic sensitivity of this unfolding chronicle makes "Events and Victims" a moving, significant document. The textual oddities and rawness of the language—indicative of a neophyte's immersion into English and a veteran activist's unfiltered scorn of exploitation and oppression—heighten the effect of the prose's power. Rather than enervating expression, this putative crudity instills not only authenticity of vision but also brings about certain expressions and grammatical figurations that elaborate a dynamic street poetry.

Moral fervor, rather than specific ideological passion, infuses the tale. In fact, despite the numerous indignant asides and negative social assessments, no argument is ever advanced specifying either a solution to injustice or a particular mode of political emancipation. The fidelity to a mostly expository presentation of materials is curious given that his letters are unstinting avowals of anarchist overthrow of the world social order. Vanzetti learned a restraint reminiscent of nineteenth-century purveyors of social realist novels, perhaps understanding that the spectacle as described would indict itself. Wavering beyond the horizon of the particular scenarios in the narrative is a concern not simply with liberation politics but the possible annihilation of the world, "the tragicomic autodestruction of the race." His stance is ethical and, repeatedly, environmental: "The good Liberians, instead of watching with philosophical inertia the invasion of the sea, think only of their seawalls and busy themselves with constructing great concrete walls along the most dangerously threatened points of the sea."

Apocalypse looms, and Vanzetti's narrator, both a stand-in for the author and perhaps autonomous in that he has no coherent politics, assumes a raw subjectivity and is continually concerned whether humanity on the verge of destruction can save itself. The narrative's tone and its violent, visceral ending makes this prospect seem unlikely, though the author himself was a partisan of hope as well as anarchist principles.

For an activist devoted to advancing the cause of anarchism, who identified the international working class as the saving grace of this enterprise, the agents of our liberation, his depiction of "the masses" can often be querulous. When the narrator goes in search of his comrade at a local movie theater, he is moved to dispense the following remark regarding mass media and the masses:

6

Of course it was, as usual, crowded to the doors. The common people, being all heart and no brain, are passionately interested in such senseless stories and not a scene escapes them. They develop a wild and unreasoning affection for the unreal characters of the unreally good whose hatreds and loves, risks and triumphs they share.

His observation of the various workers at the munitions factory can also be critical—yet not dismissive. Rather than romanticizing the working class like so many well-intentioned but woefully naive leftist commentators have done over centuries, Vanzetti exudes a clear-eyed sensibility. Descriptively, he adopts a prescriptive voice, showing that humane transformation of the work space or wider political sphere is unachievable as long as individuals are complicit in the mechanisms of their own oppression.

Indeed, the degraded, diminished social landscape Vanzetti imagines and documents remains resistant to stark satire because of the extremity of its condition. Troubling, this land of extremity is ours, unexaggerated and witheringly present. Vanzetti itemizes the various setbacks to the sisterhood and brotherhood of humankind he records time and again in his correspondence. In addition to environmental crisis, media saturation, warmongering, and general social passivity, his inventory includes the stages of dehumanization that afflict the international working class. He laments how the immigrant foraging for work has led on too many occasion to arms production, nationalism, and an inability to identify with any but one's own provincial kin:

The helots of the earth are going mad. The newspapers are rapidly increasing their circulation. The shrewd pile up fortunes. How wonderful war is! All are posing as generals, strategists, economists, statesmen, and, oh, the gorgeously colored, great ideas they are thundering forth.

But the comedy gives place to tragedy: ties of friendship and affection are severed; daggers are sharpened and revolvers caressed. Thus the beautiful, the holy war becomes another cause of dissension, hatred, and competition into which, by pressure of social conditions and their own ignorance, the workers are driven.

This relentless, heaving rhetoric is typical of "Events and Victims"—concerned not only to make inroads into its story but offering sermon after sermon; the messenger either contriving an operator's manual for social transformation or a lament about the lack of its prospect in the near future. Or both. Whatever the case, given the general state of current national and international affairs, one can sigh, with no exaggeration, that the world Vanzetti envisions is a near facsimile of our own. *Plus ça change . . .*

Upon his incarceration in 1921, Vanzetti took to working on his defense, corresponding avidly with supporters from around the world and, in particular, members of the Sacco-Vanzetti Defense Committee, founded by Aldino Feliciani. Although with "Events and Victims" he would embark on his first (and only) sustained piece of writing in English, he had already established a voice in his mother tongue for the anarchist press. While Sacco despaired of the futility of learning English more fully given his probable fate—a sentiment justified by history—and abruptly stopped his prison tutorials, Vanzetti immersed himself in learning the language, taking evening classes in Charlestown Prison and a correspondence course with a sympathetic writing teacher named Virginia MacMechan.[4] According to MacMechan, Vanzetti yearned to become "a nightingale of the English language."[5]

Over the course of his confinement, his reading was as voracious as his writing. As if to hold up a mirror to his existence, he read prison literature, such as Silvio Pellico's *My Prisons* (*Le mie prigioni*), while also rounding out his self-education with various volumes of history, philosophy, literature, science, and religion. A partial inventory of the authors Vanzetti absorbed includes Emerson, Tagore, Dante, William James, Marcus Aurelius, Ernest Renan, Proudhon, Voltaire, Darwin, Tolstoy, Hugo, and Zola. He reread Leopardi and Dante's *Divine Comedy*. Not surprisingly, most of his reading consisted of political and social texts, especially anarchists like himself—Kropotkin, Reclus, Merlino, and Malatesta, among others.[6]

Yet the creative impulse was also invested in his intellectual odyssey; his literate life behind bars was not exclusively based on furthering his education and keeping up with news of his own trial, world events (especially the rise of fascism in his native Italy), and self-questioning a broad swath of philosophical ideas. Vanzetti wanted to write, expressing a desire not to dabble but to assert himself in the realm of literature. Therefore, his learning of English occurred in conjunction with a desire to go beyond practical communication and on to narrating stories and structures of experience beyond the merely technical and personal.

In early October 1923, he wrote Upton Sinclair: "I have finished a short novel which will soon be published—at least—so I was told; and I will send a copy to you." He goes on to pardon his authorial intentions accordingly: "Please do not believe that I am conceited—I know my littleness—humble I wrote for the humble who must conquer the world to peace and freedom; and I try to make plain humble but ignored truths."[7]

To the famous novelist, Vanzetti shows due deference. To longtime supporter and sometime writing assistant Elizabeth Glendower Evans, he strikes a different tone, seeming more self-possessed, conscious of his mission to wield words, and showing a certain pride in his inadequacy using them: "My other teacher, Mrs. V.M.M., has criticise a little my 'pedantic way of writing.' I told her that is not due to pretensions of any sort, but simply and purely by my 'blessing ignorance of the English language.'"[8]

"Events and Victims" would be the only existing completed fictional work by Vanzetti, and there is no evidence from his correspondence or the inventory of his prison possessions that he made another literary effort. But rather than being a mere curio attached to an individual caught up in one of the most controversial U.S. court cases, the text highlights an authorial voice coming into its own, illuminating an imagined world based on one of harsh, lived experience—his own.

Just slightly more than a year before he was to be executed, Vanzetti stated in a postscript to a letter to Virginia MacMechan: "I am told that they burnt my anarchist journals which they found in my box in the store-house since my return from Bridgewater. By burning the symbols of thought and the thinker, they cannot destroy the thought itself—for it thrives and won in the ashes."[9]

For the most part, Vanzetti did not write for posterity, "Events and Victims" being the one possible exception. Finally, after almost a century, it now finds its way into print.

Note on the Text

Two drafts survive of "Events and Victims," the latter of which has been corrected by both an outside editor—in all likelihood Virginia MacMechan, Vanzetti's writing instructor—and Vanzetti himself. While the second draft can be considered authoritative, the original contains key phrasings and descriptions that bear preserving. Frequently, in a bid for accuracy, correctness, and standardization, Vanzetti's words have been altered, expunged, or else written over in ink with sometimes helpful suggestions for revision. However—and this is will sound toxic to anxious grammarians—I have chosen to keep included in various passages Vanzetti's signature syntax and personal, if grammatically stilted or downright incorrect, expression in the final version. My intention is to help render a writer making his first soundings in the language perceptible to the reader, while also acknowledging that even vexed, awkward diction can serve as a rough music, a vernacular patterning culminating in unlikely combinations and oblique poetic resonance. To purify the work would seem almost to stifle it, authorize a voice not entirely his own—and Vanzetti's own contempt of authority is certainly acknowledged in this editorial decision. His particular technique and vision seem fundamental, regardless of their sometimes eccentric verbal embodiments.

Of course, repetitions, useless qualifiers, and wordiness can be subdued without compromising the general structure and tone of the sentences, and correct punctuation has been put in place. Sometimes clarification is needed, as when a movie theater is described as "showing a screen version" when "screening a film" will suffice. The editorial intrusions, intermittently helpful, can often lead to unnecessary additions. "Little brain and less knowledge" has been handwritten over Vanzetti's "no brain"—referring to contemporary theatergoers—a glib, redundant choice not worth choosing.

The most expansive editorial transformation occurs at the very end of "Events and Victims," more a matter of preservation than restructuring. The final five paragraphs of draft one seem so much more complete than their draft two counterparts; with more nuance and dimension, a far more sympathetic consideration of the characters involved in the factory accident emerges. Draft two seems too scripted and abrupt, preachy in a fashion more in keeping with socialist realist novels or a Sunday sermon, departing from the narrative altogether after contemplating the main victim: "Because there is no way out: either renew or perish." This shaky curtain call had originally given witness to the dying worker and his final words: "New life . . . new life … I perish … I die." This first version might be faulted too for being stilted and melodramatic, but at least it allows the narrative autonomy to conclude without the add-on of last-minute commentary. That Vanzetti had drawn a huge box around the last sequence, presumably to mark it for excision, is odd, given its far more sensitive, powerful ending. The polemic pitch of version two seems more appropriate for the op-ed activist than the radical writer. In any case, the finalized version of "Events and Victims" sustains the frisson and imprimatur of its author, its form uniquely hybrid like him: citizen and prisoner, resident and alien, Italian and English speaker and writer.

Notes

1. The vast inventory of books read by prison writers are a useful sketch of their range of tastes, models for inspiration, imitation, or abandonment, and the relative accessibility of books and of which types.
2. The great revolutionary and writer Victor Serge sums it up perfectly in his 1930 novel *Men in Prison*: "Prison tries to stultify: to mechanize all movements, efface all character, desiccate the brain." (Richard Greeman, trans. [Oakland: PM Press, 2014], 129).
3. Conflict with Germany would suggest World War I, although Vanzetti never specifies. In light of Vanzetti's concern about fascism in his native land and its influence on greater European affairs and developments in both countries over the next two decades, the reference seems prophetic.
4. Gardner Jackson and Marion D. Frankfurter, eds., *The Letters of Sacco and Vanzetti* (New York: Penguin Books, 1997), lvii.
5. Bruce Watson, *Sacco and Vanzetti: The Men, the Murders, and the Judgment of Mankind* (New York: Viking Press, 2007), 225.
6. Paul Avrich, *Sacco and Vanzetti: The Anarchist Background* (Princeton, NJ: Princeton University Press, 1991), 35.
7. October 4, 1923. Sinclair ms. (unpublished)
8. Gardner and Frankfurter, *The Letters of Sacco and Vanzetti*, 111.
9. Gardner and Frankfurter, 197.

Events and Victims

THE EVENTS WHICH I AM GOING TO RELATE TO YOU, MY READER, TOOK place in New Liberia, where I wandered for many years, working from time to time in many different places and under varied circumstances, as dishwasher, pastry cook, porter, storekeeper, gardener, laborer, fisherman; in short, earning my bread by the sweat of my brow wherever and in whatever way I could.

The western coast of that country, according to the geologists, is being eaten by the tides, and the land slowly but inevitably yields to the restless surges which stir it, submerge and cover it. The eastern coast, too, seems subject to the same phenomenon, at least at certain points with which I am very familiar.

Will this engulfment continue, or will it be stopped by one of the many still unexplained conditions which have determined and facilitated the infinite forms of matter and of life? Will they disappear, those shores so vast, so beloved, and so desperately disputed, each bush, tree, cliff, rock, and hill of which have been so bitterly contested by a handful of men poisoned by greed and folly? What destiny has time in store for that land all possessed by a foolish and feverish human activity; strewn with shanties, slums, and mediocre houses for its idle or ill-occupied rich; with the gigantic creations of human genius and labor interwoven; with the marbles and tombs of its departed poets, sages, learned and proclaimed heroes? Or will the blind seas sacrifice that land to their greedy gorges in order that the fabled Atlantises may raise again their heads, bowed by millenniums but still desirous of the light, to the mighty caresses of the sun? Or will that land be spared to witness the tragicomic autodestruction of the race; or to become the last receptacle and final grave of degenerated tyrants, deceivers, and ruffians, and from the last hour of the darkest age—to see the clear dawn of sane and free days arise?

The good New Liberians, instead of watching with philosophical inertia the invasion of the sea, think only of their seawalls and busy themselves with constructing great concrete walls along the most dangerously threatened points of the shore.

A gang of workmen—all foreigners, from the engineer to the humblest laborer—had been busy erecting one of these walls since the beginning of spring. They had toiled so through the summer and the fall that at the beginning of winter the work was almost completed.

"Well, in a few days I will be fired; I must look for another job," I told myself one gloomy afternoon, as I watched the fog slowly stealing from me the sea, the sky, and sun.

That night instead of lying down to smoke and read, I did what I always do in such emergencies, I went to the poolroom of my friend Gennarino, a very able, intelligent, and enterprising barber. There the workingmen of the neighborhood spend their winter evenings reading, smoking, playing, disputing about politics, and chatting about work. There one may learn news of the labor market in the vicinity.

"I hear that they are looking for hands in Greenland," a friend told me soon after I entered, "but I don't know anything for sure. Johnny who works there can tell you more about it."

I went out and walked towards the theatre, hoping to see Johnny whom I knew to be passionately fond of moving picture shows. That night they were screening a film, a fragment of one of those romances which distort truth and realities; falsify history; provoke, cultivate, and embellish all the morbid emotions, confusions, ignorances, prejudices, and horrors; and purposely and skillfully pervert the hearts and, still more, the minds. The characters of these morbid melodramas are always of two opposite types, one very good, the other very bad. The good ones are the good folks who are always good, always do good, are always right, and in the end always triumph. The others are always bad folk, who are always wrong, always do evil, and finally pay the penalty. Just the reverse of life!

Thus meditating, I reached the theatre. Of course, it was, as usual, crowded to the doors. The common people, being all heart and no brain, are passionately interested in such senseless stories and not a scene escapes them. They develop a wild and unreasoning affection for the unreal characters of the unreally good, whose hatreds and loves, risks, and triumphs they share—and fervid hatred for and resentment against the unreal characters of the unreally bad gang. They lose their heads, weep, sigh, laugh, smile, fear, hope, and throb, and, forgetting their cross of infamy, leave the theatre more stupid than when they entered it. So in New Liberia.

As the first performance of the show was still going on, I stopped in front of the main entrance of the theatre and stood on the curb of the sidewalk. I felt sure that I would see Johnny come out of the show, or that he would see me, that anyway we would meet. It was still early and men and women were going back and forth doing their shopping or business or taking an evening stroll. Some were alone, some in friendly groups, a mother and her daughters, or sisters together. I silently watched them, exchanging salutations with some—all so familiar to my eyes, though so strange to me.

Beside me on the sidewalk stood a large group of men of all ages— the regular evening habitués of this particular point of the sidewalk. They looked the passing women up and down. They jokingly commented upon the age, walk, figure, face, and family relations of each woman that passed. Feeling uneasy, I turned toward the street and, almost unconsciously, I lifted my head. The fog of the afternoon had disappeared, the air was cold and clear, the sky cloudless. Beyond the foliage and the branches of two fine old trees between which I stood, some stars appeared in vast black concave of the sky. I looked at them thinking, contemplating, sensing my smallness, and, at the same time, the deepness and fullness of life: the small things and noises around my low level had faded from my consciousness.

Just then I felt a hand upon my shoulder. I turned, and there was Johnny standing beside me, looking into my face with a smile—a smile that plainly said: "You fool, to save a few nickels you deprive yourself of such pleasure as I have just enjoyed." We talked for a little and then separated. The next morning I was to start with him for Greenland.

On my way home I was churning in my mind: "What shall I do? The wages are lower than I am getting now, and furthermore thirty cents train fare and an hour longer to work daily. Damn the government! But the winter is long, and there I shall be able to work every day regardless of snow, rain, or wind. I will go."

The next morning I got to the station just in time to get my ticket and board the train. I found a seat beside Johnny, who had arrived in good season. As soon as the train started on its way, my friend began: "You see, Mr. Greenland's two factories were both closed at the beginning of the war. Now he has begun to manufacture cannon shells in one of them."

"Bombs," I interrupted.

"And now," my friend went on, "they are working day and night and turning out great quantities of them. You can't imagine what terrible work it is—water, humidity, steam, smoke, smells, heat, fire, acids: a veritable hell. The wages are good, but there are certain kinds of work that nobody wants to do."

"I understand," I mumbled.

"The factory we are going to is being used to manufacture dyes and colors. Before the war these products were brought from Germany. Now they are made here."

Seeing that I was silent, he added: "Anyhow the poor fellows are earning a living."

"Yes," said I.

I was not in a talkative mood because I felt the keen need of mental concentration. I was thinking: "There on the other side of the pond, the war rages, destroying the flower of European manhood, covering those regions once beautiful by nature and made more beautiful and wondrous by the hands and intelligence of all the bygone generations with bloody and desolate ruins."

"Here the human beings who have emigrated from the warring nations suddenly espouse the cause of those fatherlands from whence they have gladly fled in search of bread and of a new life. Those from the neutral countries are extolling to the stars their birthlands' governments, which know how to spare their peoples the scourge and the horror of this insane war.

Each of the two fighting groups is dead sure of being in the right: of having been attacked first; of being entitled to victory which will bring great advantages; while the neutrals laugh at both sides and look down from a superior height with benign compassion upon them, posing as supermen who know all things.

These disinherited of the many fatherlands, in whom the forced exodus from their native place has frozen the very tears in their hearts, they to whom everything was denied, from bread to education, when are they drawing their antagonistic opinions, their false information, their thousand errors, their equivocal reasonings, their unjustified indignation and foolish hopes; their passions, hatreds, and grotesque vainglory?

Alas, it's just because I believe I have a little knowledge of some of the sources of this evil that I am classed as a rebel and an innovator and have the time to tell you, my reader, these reminisces of mine. Instead of an interrogation to myself, the above question was rather a statement of facts brought to my mind by the logical train of thought on war matters.—But just at this point, as I glanced through the train, I saw the glaring headlines on the newspapers which everyone was devouring.

"There was my answer, in part at least—The Press. Yes, from the press which calls itself Italian, New Liberian, German, Spanish, English, French. The inciting scribblers prostituting their intelligence for the gold of those who desire war keep their pens busy concealing and perverting the truth, safely hiding their infamy behind the excited ignorance of the masses, which makes every lie possible.

The helots of the earth are going mad. The newspapers are rapidly increasing their circulation. The shrewd pile up fortunes. How wonderful war is! All are posing as generals, strategists, economists, statesmen, and, oh, the gorgeously colored, great ideas they are thundering forth.

But the comedy gives place to tragedy; ties of friendship and affections are severed; daggers are sharpened and revolvers caressed. Thus the beautiful, the holy war becomes another cause of dissension, hatred, and competition into which, by pressure of social conditions and their own ignorance, the workers are driven.

But in the New Liberians the war excites only contempt and execration. To them the peoples across the ocean, cutting each other's throats, destroying towns, fields, forests, roads, and bridges, are but stupid people of inferior minds, without ideals, hordes of barbarians, blind and docile tools in the hands of greedy kings, who use them ruthlessly to further their designs of conquest and domination by violence, fraud, and robbery.

"No," they cry, "we will never join in such a barbarous game. We, free citizens of this republic, we elected as our President, a man who has promised to keep us out of the war."

It is true! Now the nation is galvanized by pride. From his seat the President of New Liberia has proclaimed: "The New Liberians are too civilized to fight and to entrust to arms the defense of their rights. New Liberia will never take part in the war."

Marat was right when he said: "It is necessary to praise the people; it is necessary to intoxicate it by a vain exaltation of itself in order to more easily and better deceive it."

During this period, this nation is rapidly overcoming the economic crisis which has afflicted her for several years. As if by magic, old industries acquire new vigor, new ones are established and thrive, unemployment is disappearing, the labor demand is becoming urgent, wages are rising . . . but still more so are prices and profits.

Who is performing this miracle? Whence this unexpected blessing?

The War has performed the miracle. The blessing comes straight from terror-stricken cities, from the smoking ruins of villages, from devastated fields, from cold deserted hearths, from the oaths of the slayers and the curses and groans of the dying young soldiers, from rivers of blood and heaps of rotting corpses.

And here, in New Liberia, without remorse or sorrow, they are gladly taking advantage of the opportunity and feeding and equipping the War. By making the War possible they are reaping undreamed of profits and colossal fortunes.

A vigorous jolt of the train coming to a standstill tore me from my meditation.

"We are in Greenland," sighed Johnny starting for the door. On my way to the factory I looked about me. It was a wonderful morning, the air bracing and clear as crystal. Under the bright eye of the morning sun each object stood out clean-cut and vivid, and the wild Nordic panorama of the place appeared in a glory of light.

The railroad station, all red save the black roof steaming with the damp of the past night, looked like the summit of a mountain: the rails glittered like a busy ploughshare curving and disappearing into the forest; forest to the right, forest to the left. Farther on, the windows of some houses were aflame with the reflection of the morning sun glancing through the naked tree trunks and branches; and high above all, amid a strangely alive black and grey multitude of trees, loomed a distant hill and crowning it a wooden belfry topped by a cross gleaming in the sunlight and dominating over all.

This village is one of the very many industrial feudal tenures scattered amid the forests along the river's banks and the coast of New Liberia. It bears the name of the Overlord who owns by law the two churches, the two factories, and almost all the houses and the soil itself. I leave it to your imagination, my reader, what may belong to the Overlord by arbitration or even by desire—if, from your knowledge of the ancient feudalism of the old nobility in the name of God, you can deduce the possibility of this actual feudalism of the present-day bourgeois in the name of the law.

When we reached the main entry, John pushed the door open and quickly closed it behind us as we crossed the threshold. What a difference from outside: I felt an instinctive impulse to flee—to return to the sunshine and life-giving air, blessed and pure. But I resisted and followed John, who, after a few steps, stopped in front of the superintendent's office and said: "I am going to work, you wait here and when Mr. D— comes in, ask him for a job."

I waited and while waiting I examined my surroundings. Inside the entry there was a hall about thirty-six feet long and about half as high as the building. A door and a window opened on the left wall—both looking into the superintendent's office. The right wall was blind. The long hall led into a great room with small windows, and in it was a crane on wheels running from one end to the other.

This was the factory.

Barrels and demijohns reinforced by wooden frames were piled up here and there. In the rear, the floor was coated with cement. Here stood two huge wooden tanks about fifteen feet high with platforms and iron railings round them. Wooden steps led to the platform. The enormous covers of the tanks were suspended over them by fixed cranes. Metal pipes of various dimensions were to be seen all around. A very long rubber hose lay along the floor.

Human figures covered with dirt and wearing high wet boots and rubber gloves were moving round the tanks.

While I was observing everything intently, Mr. D— entered his office. Presently he came out and looked at me enquiringly.

"Have you any work for a laborer?" I asked.

"I need men for the tanks. I pay them ten cents an hour more than the other laborers."

"I don't want to work at the tanks."

He started to go, then stopped, made a half turn, glanced at his watch, and said:

"Go work with the laborers."

***

The old wooden floor had to be replaced by a new one of concrete; raw materials and new machinery had to be unloaded, manufactured goods and empty vessels had to be shipped. All of which was entrusted to the laborers. The timber from the old floor, which was still usable, had to be removed and piled up beyond the factory, while that which was useless had to be taken to a little creek in the wood nearby where the drainage water flowed in a lazy stream which every few steps made a little pool and then resumed its feeble journey.

I soon realized that if the other factory was, in John's words: "a veritable hell," the extreme limit of purgatory.

There was not a mouse in the factory, not an insect on the woods and waters nearby. Even the birds kept far away from it and circled it in their flight, as a ship steers round a danger spot, or soared high above it. The vegetation all around was dead or withering.

It is civilization, it is prosperity—which Johnny says "makes the paupers live"—that projects poisons into the air and water driving out everything that is not artificial. But can man—man who is the most sensitive and delicate of creatures—thrive and rise where the very birds, mice, insects, and plants are unable to exist?

***

The foreman was a New Liberian of gigantic stature. He had the simple mentality, the habits, the manners of a man born and raised in a village. Unfit as he evidently was for the surroundings of a modern industrial plant, which grinds and subordinates everything to profit—he must have got his position through "pull." He was slow, inexperienced, incapable of harnessing the workers, and good at heart. We treated him well and tried to make up for his inexperience by our industry. He was amused and laughed at the many ingenious devices with which the experienced worker multiplies his physical strength and motions, and, watching our calculations of time and motion, he wondered how we laborers had learned in the practical school of life those elementary principles of physics and mechanics which we had not had time and opportunity to learn in schools.

And yet sometimes the luminous eyes of this simple giant became cold when observing me. He had heard so many wild tales, so many horrible stories, about these "foreigners," who smiled at him and with whom he had come in contact for the first time. He hardly understood himself his vague feeling of distrust, something beyond his own power to analyze, something intangible, instilled into him a sort of fear, a repugnance, a hatred which strangely intermingled with his lack of mental strength to understand. At moments it seemed that they might be good men, then again, because he had not always known them, he thought it must be impossible that they should be good, and yet he could not point out even to himself in what way they were bad.

They were "foreigners," that was enough, that was the answer.

At about two o'clock in the afternoon a thick greenish fume began to rise from the tanks, rising to the ceiling and then floating down again in a cloud-like mass. From this and from the tanks themselves emanated an irritating odor of sulphuric acid gas stifling and choking the workers and burning their eyes. Soon tears were streaming from my smarting eyes, and I asked the man next to me if they were manufacturing dyes or asphyxiating gases.

Coughing violently, and with his eyes closed, he answered: "Wait, and you will find out."

I did not have to wait long. A layer of fumes rose and covered the whole of the ceiling of the factory, then gradually descended to meet a new cloud rising from the tank. The cloud grew thicker and thicker. The thicker it got and the nearer it came, the greater was our suffering. There were convulsive coughs on every side, the tears poured from the eyes, and finally we were all coughing and crying. The men at the tanks quit their work and hurried away, followed by the carpenters working near them. Handing over our shovels, we stopped work also, as it was impossible to keep our eyes open. The windows were flung open but without result—we got no relief, our suffering became unbearable, the fumes choked us and burned our eyes until we were frantic. Coughing, weeping, blinded, gasping, groping, we went back to the door. Here we stopped, hesitating, until a puff of the pestiferous exhalation almost overcame us. At last we threw open the door and rushed into the open.

***

Now that the "men of the tanks" were near to me, I had a chance to observe them. I scrutinized each one, I tried to understand them. It was not so difficult to understand their thoughts and emotions at that moment. They were New Liberian farmers who had quit the soil for the factory, yielding to the spell exercised by the fascination of the town upon their naive mentality, urged by the occult social factors which they unconsciously obeyed. Under the sincere sunlight they looked more haggard than they appeared in the factory. Pale, emaciated, dirty—a pitiful lot—yet upon their countenance were deep lines of strong determination and great hopes. These sentiments were written all over them, even in their gestures. That in their minds were dancing fascinating dreams of glories and great fortunes was as evident as the poisoning of their cells that caused their ghastly appearance.

They were repeating to themselves: "Thus, even as we, and maybe still lower, many men have begun whose fame and wealth the world is now bowing down to. Ah yes, it takes hard work, strength of will, perseverance, self-denial, the spirit of sacrifice, to become rich and powerful."

Knowing that we had refused to work at the tanks and were satisfied with our lower wages, and, worse, satisfied to wield the shovel which they already cordially despised, it was plain that they held us in contempt as "cowards." They did not say so, they kept silent but let it be understood by that very silence, the very air seemed to echo: "Cowards, you will always be miserable."

"Yes, it is true," my thoughts answered their looks, "we will always be miserable, indeed always more miserable, as long as we do not know how to ameliorate ourselves and find the impetus, the courage, and the strength to conquer and master our own destiny. But in a premature grave you poor cheated fools will witness the wreckage of your absurd hopes and false faith, while physical weakness, multiplied vices, false sentiments, and oppression will be the only heritage that fate, shaped by your own folly and that of others, reserves for your children."

What perversion: how far they have strayed in so short a time.

Who ignores what happened in the latter part of the eighteenth century when the great industries at their inception called for service which no one was willing to give? Who ignores the violence which, after vain promises and allurements, proved fruitless, was used to drive the peasantry from the country to the city, to compel them to leave the loved furrows and give the strength of their arms to the new machinery? To become twice slaves—slaves of the masters and slaves of the new machines! Who ignores the intervention of the law which first deprived them of their fields by the abolition of the communal lands, then condemned to the gallows the rebellious peasants it had forced into vagabondage—and the bloody rebellions of these same peasants, bloody with their own blood alone?

And yet these ancient peasants showed a heroic resistance. Because they loved their fields, their independence, the northeast wind, as well as the dog days, and under the blazing sun and the lash of the elements had grown sane and normal, exuberant with love. They instinctively felt and clearly thought that in the cities and factories people lost health both of body and soul.

Finally, having been deprived of their lands, compelled to a vagrancy punishable by the gallows, they submitted and went to the cities, to the factories—to physical and moral aberrations.

But ever since these days a great dream of redemption, token of a radiant future, has flourished in the spirits of the vanquished. And only by the realization of that dream, which will abrogate every unjust mortgage upon the rights and the value of life, do the vanquished expect to attain that place assigned by nature to every man born of woman at the banquet of life.

But now, and here, these arch-conceited villains, docile descendants of brave and rebellious grandparents, are abandoning their own fields, liberty, and health to run to the factory in a mad attempt to attain wealth.... Why?

***

A man appeared at the gate to tell us that we might return to our work. We silently obeyed. Each one resumed his task.

***

It is customary for every experienced laborer, when new on a job, to imitate the methods, habits, and conduct of the older workers. This is the only way to avoid being abused by the foreman, to preserve the rights acquired in the conflicts between masters and slaves, and also to escape the bitter rebuke of the other workers.

The next morning, following the rule, I observed whatever the workers did. Thus, imitating them, I was given a pair of new gloves and was much surprised to see the men seizing their shovels and cleaning them with great care. They scrubbed and scraped the handles as hard as they could, using a scraper that they afterwards threw away. Wondering at this, I asked the reason for such unusual cleanliness.

"Do you see this greenish layer of dust on the shovel? It is poison. This is dangerous business, watch out, take care. Get new gloves every morning; clean your shovel thoroughly; clean your hands carefully before touching anything to eat. At the slightest scratch run to the drugstore. You see we are working among the most dangerous poisons of all time. Remember, and do as I tell you as long as you work here."

I thanked him.

***

Several weeks passed without accident except the daily exhalation of sulphuric acid and a few comic episodes arising from the obstinacy of the laborers concerning the work about the tanks. One morning we noticed several pipes turned and others broken to pieces around the tanks and the traces of an abundant use of water. A strange silence reigned in the factory. What had happened during the night work? A calamity? Had that water been used to cleanse the floor of human blood? I shall never know.

A few days afterward something happened, which, though apparently insignificant, was soon to cut off an exuberant young life, to whom the future was smiling with the fascination of a thousand illusions.

To explain this happening, I must go back a little. From the first day of my arrival, my attention had been attracted by the queer ways of one of the men. He was a handsome youth of about twenty-seven years, of rather short stature but broad-shouldered, strong, and agile. His dress was something between a clerk and a laborer. He spoke to no one. He moved quickly, often passing his hands through his thick hair when it hung down in his face, and if his hands were occupied, he would toss it back from his forehead with a beautiful energetic movement of his head.

For several days I tried to find out what his regular trade was, but without success. I saw him move about, stopping here and there to wield furiously the pick, shovel, or hammer—strike a great blow to the right, another to the left, then drop the tool as if it were burning his hands.

He handled all kinds of tools in succession, changing places and work with surprising restlessness. An old laborer easily recognized the symptoms. Alfred—this was his name—was a job hunter, morally faithless. As with all adventurers, he was trusting to dishonesty, legal or otherwise, to get the leisure, the comforts, and satisfactions which the honest worker cannot afford. Not sufficiently ignorant to share with the simpleminded folk the childish hope of an equitable reward for labor; not sufficiently educated to be familiar with the natural law of compensation; unwilling to work and without an independent income, he could only depend on evil, which he did. He thought he saw a chance to "rise" to "get ahead." The time and place were propitious.

He was sure that Germany would be utterly defeated and that New Liberia would inherit leadership in the production of chemicals. If anyone had told him that within a few years the New Liberian barons of the new industry would have to engage lobbyists and politicians to obtain protective tariffs and laws in order to withstand the competition of German products—Alfred would have thought him crazy.

"Here, it is possible to get a good position," he was thinking. It was sufficient for him to show that he had no scruples, no human respect for the less fit than he, in order to prove that he knew how to use authority and command. At last he was wearing his first laurels!

The first laurels . . . ! He had succeeded in supplanting the old foreman who thus became a plain laborer!

But this man so harshly treated knew how to conceal his internal suffering. Only a slight paleness, an unnatural brightness of his blue eyes that gradually grew colder, and a repressed tremor that shook his huge body—the most cruel form of weeping—whispered of the battle within.

The sorrow and shame of a man who had himself the sincerity and virtue of an era which is disappearing, awakened our pity. That evening, in his home, the giant wept like a child, and with him wept his old aunt, a spinster who had been a mother to him.

That same evening Alfred was kissed by his young wife as the brave and victorious are rewarded—he was fighting and winning his way upward.

And we realized that we had lost out in the change.

***

The next morning Alfred arrived at the factory confident and happy, this time in command. Also the blue-eyed giant had arrived, but to be commanded, to take orders, to obey. And to be commanded for the first time, at his age; to be commanded, he, with white hair, whose ancestors had fought for the glory and independence of the fatherland, commanded by a despised intruder from across the border. This was too much for a man who sincerely believed himself to belong to the elect, the people pre-elected by God and nature; to a race for whose benefit and service the semi-human rabble, the nameless, graceless hordes driven by hunger, misfortune, and ignorance to the sacred shore of his native land, had been created.

Sleepless and sorrowful, he had passed the night recalling, understanding, and realizing all the perfidy and trickery by which Alfred had supplanted him, feeling ridiculed, humiliated, offended. A mortal hatred seized him. He tried in vain to hide his anguish under the cloak of an external calm. We saw him turn pale as he picked up his shovel to start with us to heavy labor.

Alfred was determined to show his superiority over his predecessor by trying from the first hour to make us work harder than before. He had laid his plan of procedure.

That day cement was being prepared for the new floor. The new boss seized a tub of water and began to pour it into the material as fast as he could, knowing that the material must be fixed as fast as the water is poured. By setting a fast pace he intended to force us to do likewise.

Laughing at the way he not only soaked the men around him but also himself, we exchanged knowing looks.

The days had passed when a tremendous labor crisis rendered the "meat work" the most despised, turned the workers out of their huts, deprived them of their daily bread, forced them to prostitution, espionage, crime, and suicide. The beautiful war, the holy war, had relegated all that to the memories of the accursed past. We exchanged knowing, planning looks. We were not afraid to lose our poor jobs. Were we not sought after, respected, appreciated, petted, and flattered? Did we not seem to live among different people in a different world? The rabble had not forgotten the insults, the ineradicable sufferings, and everywhere it took advantage of the favorable opportunity and revenged itself by returning worse for evil to the slave-driving foreman, and by doing so slow, careless work in place of their former bestial toil.

"It is very undignified—in fact dishonorable," someone strong in morals may observe.

Undignified—true, but not dishonorable. Can the slaves be blamed if they have been defrauded of common sense and dignity? "Of the natural sense," as Marat used to say. And if they had not been thus defrauded, would they be slaves at all?

To one who warned them that a historical tragedy had been started and not a carnival; that by working they were making themselves accomplices of the masters and tyrants; that no one would be spared; that darker and more ferocious future would be unemployment, hunger, shame, and desperation—the slaves replied that the war will disclose to the lucky survivors (among whom, of course, each

30

was sure he would be) an earthly paradise. And to one who insisted upon teaching them replied: "Is it possible that you, a ragamuffin like ourselves, presume to think that you know more and better than the storekeeper, the barber, the journalists, the preachers, the kings and ministers, and the president himself?"

But to return to the facts—slaves are so accustomed to toil that they worked even harder than the interest of the owners and the Society for the Prevention of Cruelty to Animals would have allowed horses to work. Never before in history was the sweat of slaves more vain for themselves, more productive to the slave drivers.

Well, reader, I have gone off the beaten track, but the conditions and reasons exposed in this digression are just the conditions and the reasons which brought about our agreement to play a practical joke on our new foreman and to escape punishment.

Instead of keeping up with Alfred's speed, we did just the opposite and began to mix the material very slowly, so that Alfred soon saw that he had poured in too much water. Then he ordered us to add more cement and sand, and we purposely added too much, and more water was required, and the joke would have continued if Alfred, understanding the ill feeling, had not gone away followed by our jeers of derision.

He had certainly made a bad start, but scorn was not sufficient to cure him. Alfred was not bad at heart, it was simply that he had to "get ahead" and make his career by tormenting, or seeming to torment, his underlings. He thought that the way to succeed was the show of authority. It made him feel big and powerful and he thought it would make him look as he felt. He proudly looked upon his recent promotion as the first step toward success. Young, sufficiently educated, he anticipated a far better position than his present one if, of course, he knew how to play his present role. His duty, he believed, was to behave as he had done that morning. He had a lovely young wife who made him very happy, and their baby, beautiful as love, was just blessing them with its first smiles.

For this women's sake, for the sake of their child, Alfred was unjust to his fellow men. Worse than wicked, he was unconscious of the urge which compelled him to seek the happiness of his beloved ones at the expense of other men's happiness.

Whose fault, if not that of present-day society based on competition and antagonism, which compelled him to play the role of either wolf or lamb, as well as everywhere else one must be either wolves or lambs?

***

During the weeks following the day of his promotion some of the men contracted the dreadful infection of which I had been so carefully warned by my fellow worker.

It began with small white blisters between the fingers and toes, then the skin began to break out in an eruption which spread gradually to the forearms, the armpits, the breast, and finally invaded the whole body causing swelling and an almost intolerable, consistent itching. Some were so seriously affected that they had to undergo medical treatment for several months. However, in spite of this fact, the number of laborers increased because the winter season was driving them, as it had driven me, from their regular work. They were glad to get any kind of work rather than remain idle through the winter.

Production was being increased, and more raw materials and new machinery were necessary, so that, in order to accomplish many different operations at the same time, the men were sometimes divided into gangs. In such emergencies one of the gangs was entrusted to the ex-foreman, whom, to tell the truth, the superior officer never compelled to work with us. On the contrary, under one pretext and another they tried to keep him away from us. But he was so outraged and offended that he disdained their efforts and kept with us for sheer hostility.

Sometimes we were detailed to work outside the factory, away from the direct surveillance of the head officer. Then Alfred would reveal himself. He would change his manner and seem to say: "I am not as bad as you believe me; this is the world we live in and that is the role I must play; that is all there is to it." And he would pass a package of cigarettes around.

***

More than a month after his promotion, Alfred, one fine morning in January, left the superintendent's office and with a determined expression and rapid step came to us who were mixing cement. He picked out some of us and ordered us to follow him. We went out and walked toward a freight car near which a Slav driver was waiting holding the reins of two horses to a wagon.

The company's private track reached almost to the gate of the factory, but many years of disuse had made it almost unfit for use, therefore the freight cars had to be stopped at some distance from the factory. This freight car was loaded with machinery parts which were to be taken to the factory. Alfred's face, voice, words, gestures, everything about him showed plainly that he was overexcited, dominated by a fixed idea to the point of obsession.

Why? It was very simple to understand. When ordering him to do that work the superintendent had taken out his watch to look at the time. Most likely he did it automatically, through force of habit, but Alfred gave to the possibly unconscious gesture a wholly different interpretation and was terribly agitated by it.

In little things, as in big, the slaves are, as a rule, and rightly so, hostile to their master and their commands. But there are cases in which owing to either collective aberrations or personal unexpressed interests—or things held to be so—they surpass in their zeal the most optimistic expectations of those in command.

Such was our case.

Alfred took hold of a hand truck with such wholehearted earnestness that we believed he had determined to get one wagonload to the factory before noon and we helped him willingly. Before twelve o'clock one wagonload was not only in the factory but unloaded. At one, the whistle found us in the freight car ready to begin work again.

There were just about two more loads left in the car, as the most stupid of laborers would have easily seen, and we had four hours ahead of us in which to finish the job. It could have easily been done in three hours and, after all, the object was to empty it that day to save the demurrage. Obsessed by the desire to show off, to prove his ability to turn out work, Alfred seemed to be possessed by a devil. Instead of attending to their work, the men were compelled to watch out for the safety of their feet and legs, which were constantly endangered by Alfred's frantic efforts.

John and I went to the opposite end of the car to take down a heavy steel beam. Suddenly Alfred ordered us to stop work even though the wagon was little more than half full, leaving more material in the car than could be taken in one load and not nearly enough for two. But Alfred did not reason, he ordered us to start for the factory. Thirty minutes later we were back in the car.

"All hands here," he commanded, as he placed a hand truck beside a very heavy block. With an "all together" effort of muscle and will, the block was hoisted upon the wagon. Another still heavier block was placed beside the first. On top of these a steel axle was placed and in the spaces between some lighter pieces. Evidently Alfred had determined to empty the car with this single trip of the wagon, but, seeing at last the absurdity of the idea, he changed his plan and, in order to make us forget his harshness and stupidity, took out a package of cigarettes and passed it around.

The New Liberian giant turned his back refusing the offer with a disdainful growl. The rest of us smoked and laughed at Alfred's foolishness. There were only a few pieces of metal left in the car and the wagon was overloaded.

Alfred threw away the stub of his cigarette, got on the wagon and ordered us to follow him. Seeing that I remained in the freight car, he asked me if I was afraid to get on the wagon.

"Certainly, I am," I answered, "the wagon is overloaded." He smiled and gave orders to start. John and I feared for those who were in the wagon, and we followed on foot a short distance behind. The wagon wheels creaked and groaned ominously on over the road which has been made rough and uneven by the sudden frost which had followed several warm days of rain.

When the wagon reached the level of the northeast corner of the factory and was turning toward the gate, the laborers, judging it safer, jumped off. At the gate the driver made the horses turn so that that he could back them into the factory. This action was taken for good reasons, the first being to avoid the risk of the horses being hurt or frightened by the sight of the pieces of machinery picked up by the cranes passing over their heads and, secondly, on account of the narrowness of the place.

The Slav driver maneuvered with such admirable skill that the wagon was soon in the desired position. The ex-foreman had jumped off with the others. Only Alfred remained in the wagon so that he would be ready the moment the crane got in position to start to unload.

The driver backed his horses and the wagon into the gateway, but in doing so he bumped against one of the walls. The space was very narrow, and it was extremely difficult to handle the horses. Three times he urged the horses forward, and so many times backed them, without succeeding in crossing the hall.

Both driver and horses grew more and more nervous. Alfred was on the wagon, his eyes fixed on the crane. No one was paying any attention to him. As nothing had happened coming along on the rough road, there seemed no reason to fear an accident on a smooth concrete pavement.

The driver again got his horses in the right position and in a voice of thunder shouted to them to start, but the team had been badly trained and made a jump forward, which shook the wagon dangerously.

At a still more imperative shout from the driver, the team bounded forward causing the wagon wheels to strike so violently against the threshold, which was slightly raised above the level of the pavement, that the bolts securing the body and the loaded frame started to slide off.

Alfred turned pale but with admirable presence of mind and agility got on his feet and slid backward on to floor unhurt. He tried to get out of the way of the falling load, but in stepping back he hit his shoulder against the big chain of the crane. The poor fellow in his fear and excitement did not realize the nature of the obstacle, for instead of pushing it aside and going ahead, he stopped, stared in terror at the falling load, and then jumped against the wall shoving his shoulder against it as though he would push it out of the way. But evidently he did not feel safe, for he made another convulsive movement, hit his foot against a shovel standing against the wall, stumbled, and fell on his back near the truck.

Then he tried to master his terror. A fatal victory. If he had continued to be terror-ridden, he might have intuitively rolled over and escaped danger. But the effort he made to control his mental faculties had paralyzed his body, and for an instant, while the enormous load of steel was about to fall, he remained motionless, conscious of his imminent and horrible doom. Without a movement of his white face his eyes grew serene and turned upward.

Speechless, nailed to the ground by horror and impotence, following his every move, I longed to cry out to him to roll over, but my throat would not emit a sound.

A dull heavy noise made the ground tremble. The noise was followed by a tremendous metallic vibration as from an impact of iron against iron, then a moment of deathlike silence broken by an indescribable scream of pain and despair. Alfred was supine on the floor, the three heavy steel beams across his legs smashing his thighs and groin.

His legs were broken, but it must have been the excruciating pain in his groin that made Alfred scream and scream again.

The New Liberian carpenters working near, to whom I called with all my might, and who must have heard Alfred's screams, thinking the victim was only a "foreign laborer," kept on hammering and made no move.

My fellow laborers who had witnessed the accident seemed as powerless to move as I. At last I was able to rush to the poor lad and, seizing hold of the beam across his groin, succeeded in raising it. At my side the New Liberian giant suddenly appeared and grasping the second beam seemed to be trying to raise it.

To my amazement I saw that this Hercules could not lift the weight. I looked at him again and understood—he was enjoying the intense suffering of his enemy. Naturally good, brought up on the Bible and the Golden Rule, even in a moment like this he could not forgive the affront he had received at Alfred's hands.

All these reactions to this inhuman situation passed through me in an instant and seemed to fill me with superhuman strength. With a terrific effort I succeeded in getting my knee under the beam I was already holding, while I seized with my left hand the beam that the giant refused to lift.

After what seemed an eternity, the carpenters, at last recognizing Alfred's voice, rushed to his aid and lifted the last beam from his feet.

Silently the poor creature raised himself to a sitting posture and supporting himself by his hands spread out behind him on the floor, he dragged himself slowly from under the beams.

From the waist down he was a mass of broken bones and tortured flesh, a deadly pallor spread over his young face without altering his beautiful features. He no longer lamented. His life was ebbing fast, and thoughts of his beloved wife and child, his old mother, and his shattered dreams harrowed his soul.

Superior to the torture of his flesh, the torture of his soul rendered him silent. The approach of death seemed to reveal all that Alfred might have been. A dignity worthy of man, a serenity of face, a poise of soul, all seemed to be expressed in those last moments, before the virility of those eyes should be gone forever.

***

The next day at work our minds were full of the hideous tragedy. Each man of us was imagining himself in Alfred's place at the terrifying moment when he faced sudden and awful death; in the eternity when he lay crushed and screaming beneath the heavy steel planks; in the heart rending moment when he must have faced the awful truth— that the beloved wife and child for whom he was struggling would be without a protector and that it was his own greedy folly that had swept him out of the world.

When we had time to think and, at last, to talk it all over between ourselves, sorry though we were for our fellow creature, sorry for his stricken loved ones—nearly every one of us agreed that it was better that—with his misdirected struggle to get ahead of those who really work—he should have been killed rather than a real worker. And this would surely have happened before Alfred would have been brought to a realization of his reckless madness to get ahead.

And I . . . ? I thought much! His death, of course, was as incidental as the millions of deaths on the battlefields of war and industry. But I seemed to read far more than mere death of a man in this event. By a vast association of ideas, some of which I have expressed in this narrative, and of comparisons, I saw in this mildly striving youth—Alfred—not only a victim but a symbol. The symbol of humanity.

At the very last moment of life Alfred's face had become distorted and inhuman, as had his voice, and the words which he tried to scream forth likewise seemed a symbol and a warning, though it was caused by the destroying agony of the pain in his groin: "New life . . . new life . . . I perish . . . I die."

THE END

BARTOLOMEO VANZETTI WAS BORN IN 1888 IN VILLAFALLETTO, Italy. As an immigrant anarchist, he was at the center of one of the most notorious legal cases of the twentieth century, along with Nicola Sacco, that highlighted American anti-immigrant and anti-radical sentiment during the Red Scare. He was executed by the Commonwealth of Massachusetts on August 23, 1927.

JON CURLEY IS A POET AND TEACHER. HIS POETRY COLLECTIONS include *Hybrid Moments* (2015) and *Scorch Marks* (2017). He also wrote *Poets and Partitions: Confronting Communal Identities in Northern Ireland* (2011) and coedited *The Poetry and Poetics of Michael Heller: A Nomad Memory* (2015). He teaches in the Humanities Department of the New Jersey Institute of Technology. Curley is originally from Bridgewater, Massachusetts, where Vanzetti's legal persecution began.

PM Press was founded at the end of 2007 by a small collection of folks with decades of publishing, media, and organizing experience. PM Press co-conspirators have published and distributed hundreds of books, pamphlets, CDs, and DVDs. Members of PM have founded enduring book fairs, spearheaded victorious tenant organizing campaigns, and worked closely with bookstores, academic conferences, and even rock bands to deliver political and challenging ideas to all walks of life. We're old enough to know what we're doing and young enough to know what's at stake.

We seek to create radical and stimulating fiction and non-fiction books, pamphlets, T-shirts, visual and audio materials to entertain, educate, and inspire you. We aim to distribute these through every available channel with every available technology, whether that means you are seeing anarchist classics at our bookfair stalls; reading our latest vegan cookbook at the café; downloading geeky fiction e-books; or digging new music and timely videos from our website.

PM Press is always on the lookout for talented and skilled volunteers, artists, activists, and writers to work with. If you have a great idea for a project or can contribute in some way, please get in touch.

PM Press
PO Box 23912
Oakland CA 94623
510-658-3906
www.pmpress.org

Friends of PM

These are indisputably momentous times—the financial system is melting down globally and the Empire is stumbling. Now more than ever there is a vital need for radical ideas.

In the many years since its founding—and on a mere shoestring—PM Press has risen to the formidable challenge of publishing and distributing knowledge and entertainment for the struggles ahead. With hundreds of releases to date, we have published an impressive and stimulating array of literature, art, music, politics, and culture. Using every available medium, we've succeeded in connecting those hungry for ideas and information to those putting them into practice.

Friends of PM allows you to directly help impact, amplify, and revitalize the discourse and actions of radical writers, filmmakers, and artists. It provides us with a stable foundation from which we can build upon our early successes and provides a much-needed subsidy for the materials that can't necessarily pay their own way. You can help make that happen—and receive every new title automatically delivered to your door once a month—by joining as a Friend of PM Press. And, we'll throw in a free T-Shirt when you sign up.

Here are your options:
- $30 a month: Get all books and pamphlets plus 50% discount on all webstore purchases
- $40 a month: Get all PM Press releases plus 50% discount on all webstore purchases
- $100 a month: Superstar—Everything plus PM merchandise, free downloads, and 50% discount on all webstore purchases

For those who can't afford $30 or more a month, we have *Sustainer Rates* at $15, $10 and $5. Sustainers get a free PM Press T-shirt and a 50% discount on all purchases from our website.

Your Visa or Mastercard will be billed once a month, until you tell us to stop. Or until our efforts succeed in bringing the revolution around. Or the financial meltdown of Capital makes plastic redundant. Whichever comes first.

Divide and Conquer or Divide and Subdivide?
How Not to Refight the First International
Mark Leier
$5.95 • ISBN: 978-1-62963-383-1

The battles between Michael Bakunin and Karl Marx in the First International (aka the International Working Men's Association, 1864–1876) began a pattern of polemics and rancor between anarchists and Marxists that still exists today. Outlining the profound similarities between Bakunin and Marx in their early lives and careers as activists, Mark Leier suggests that the differences have often been exaggerated and have prevented activists from learning useful lessons about creating vibrant movements.

Heart X-rays
A Modern Epic Poem
Marcus Colasurdo and G.H. Mosson
$5.95 • ISBN: 978-1-62963-513-2

Heart X-rays is a twenty-first-century beat epic poem that ranges across landscapes and voices, with appearances by Banksy, Pussy Riot, hip-hop, the down and out, the up and coming, heartbreak and joybreak, while exploring the mystery we call the human heart.

If indeed poetry can offer an RX, a prescription to the bloody joyful teary-eyed American paradox, it is one that calls forth all the voices that have not yet been heard, that harbors an innocence that reaches into the very heart of our own excellence. A collaborative work between two poets and working-class activists, *Heart X-rays* is a poetic memory of today written in the alphabet of a future.

Anarchy and the Sex Question
Essays on Women and Emancipation, 1896-1926
Emma Goldman • Edited by Shawn P. Wilbur
$14.95 • 978-1-62963-144-8

For Emma Goldman, the "High Priestess of Anarchy," anarchism was "a living force in the affairs of our life, constantly creating new conditions," but "the most elemental force in human life" was something still more basic and vital: sex.

"The Sex Question" emerged for Goldman in multiple contexts, and we find her addressing it in writing on subjects as varied as women's suffrage, "free love," birth control, the "New Woman," homosexuality, marriage, love, and literature. It was at once a political question, an economic question, a question of morality, and a question of social relations.

But her analysis of that most elemental force remained fragmentary, scattered across numerous published (and unpublished) works and conditioned by numerous contexts. *Anarchy and the Sex Question* draws together the most important of those scattered sources, uniting both familiar essays and archival material, in an attempt to recreate the great work on sex that Emma Goldman might have given us. In the process, it sheds light on Goldman's place in the history of feminism.

> "Emma Goldman left a profound legacy of wisdom, insight, and passionate commitment to life. Shawn Wilbur has carefully selected her best writings on that most profound, pleasurable, and challenging of topics: sex. This collection is a great service to anarchist, feminist, and queer communities around the world."
> —Jamie Heckert, coeditor of *Anarchism & Sexuality: Ethics, Relationships and Power*